WOMEN'S ROLES IN
RELIGION

Essential Viewpoints

WOMEN'S ROLES IN
RELIGION

BY MARCIA AMIDON LUSTED

Content Consultant
Lynn Ross-Bryant, PhD
Religious Studies
University of Colorado, Boulder

ABDO
Publishing Company

CREDITS

Published by ABDO Publishing Company, 8000 West 78th Street, Edina, Minnesota 55439. Copyright © 2011 by Abdo Consulting Group, Inc. International copyrights reserved in all countries. No part of this book may be reproduced in any form without written permission from the publisher. The Essential Library™ is a trademark and logo of ABDO Publishing Company.

Printed in the United States of America,
North Mankato, Minnesota
052010
092010

 THIS BOOK CONTAINS AT LEAST 10% RECYCLED MATERIALS.

Editor: Mari Kesselring
Copy Editor: Paula Lewis
Interior Design and Production: Kazuko Collins
Cover Design: Kazuko Collins

Library of Congress Cataloging-in-Publication Data
Lüsted, Marcia Amidon.
  Women's roles in religion / Marcia Amidon Lusted.
      p. cm. — (Essential viewpoints)
  Includes bibliographical references and index.
  ISBN 978-1-61613-527-0
  1. Women in religion—United States. 2. United States—Religion.
I. Title.
  BL2525.L87 2011
  200.82—dc22

                              2010002742

TABLE OF CONTENTS

The Reverend Dr. Cynthia L. Hale delivers a sermon at the Ray of Hope Church in Atlanta, Georgia.

WOMEN AND RELIGION

Women practice their religions in many different ways throughout the United States. An ordained female minister of the United Church of Christ leads a regular Sunday church worship service. A woman working as a pastoral administrator of the Catholic Church visits a sick church member in the hospital. An orthodox Jewish wife and mother gets ready for the Sabbath according to traditional rules. A woman who participates in the Wiccan religion is involved in a ceremony to honor the goddess. All of these women, whether they are participating in a ritual that has been passed down through many generations or following a new role only recently opened to them, play an important part in celebrating their faith and sharing it with others.

EQUALITY VS. TRADITION

In the twenty-first century, women in the United States have more employment opportunities than ever. In almost every way, they are achieving equality with men in the workplace and the home. In religion, however, equality between men and women has often been contested. While some religions have recently allowed women a greater role in church participation and

Understanding Feminism

Feminism is the belief that women's opportunities and rights should be equal to men's opportunities and rights. This comes from the belief that most societies currently work as patriarchies. A patriarchy is a society in which men are the sole authority figures. A feminist is a person, male or female, who disagrees with a patriarchal society. A feminist also disagrees with a matriarchal society, in which women would have all the power. They believe men and women should have equal rights and opportunities. However, feminists disagree over the best way to achieve this goal.

administration, others have held steadfastly to the traditionally defined divisions in the roles of men and women.

In some religions, women fulfill the same roles that their mothers and grandmothers followed. In other denominations, women fill positions once held only by men. Overall, the trend in most religions has been toward equality and inclusion for women in every aspect of the church. But there are still religions—and women who belong to them—that firmly believe women should maintain traditional roles as followers, not leaders, of their faith.

Worldwide, approximately 12 percent of the world's population is classified as being nonreligious. That means that the majority of people belong to a specific religious denomination. More than 78 percent of U.S. adults consider themselves Christians, 1.7 percent

Anne Nicol Gaylor

Anne Nicol Gaylor co-founded the Freedom From Religion Foundation with her daughter, Annie Laurie Gaylor, in 1976. Anne Nicol Gaylor was an atheist, which means she did not believe in any god. She also believed that religion was one of the major reasons behind the oppression of women. She felt that without religion, women would stand a better chance of becoming liberated.

The foundation and Gaylor have filed numerous lawsuits to support their strong belief in the separation of church and state. One lawsuit attempted to prevent President Ronald Reagan from naming 1983 as the year of the Bible. The foundation also worked to remove Bibles from some hotel and motel rooms.

*Women marched in support of women's rights
in New York City on August 26, 1970.*

are Jewish, and 0.6 percent follow the religion of
Islam. In many religious denominations, women
make up at least half—and sometimes more—of
the members. From social service and outreach
programs to administrative duties and worship
leadership, women play extremely important roles
in the functioning of their religions. However, some
women feel undervalued by their religions while
others are content with filling traditional roles.

According to June Melby Benowitz in the *Encyclopedia of American Women and Religion*,

> At present, many religious denominations in the United States continue to be [male-dominated]. . . . The majority of women . . . [seek] greater influence and power within their religious denominations, but others [are] content to maintain subordinate roles.[1]

The Woman's Bible

In 1895, suffrage leader Elizabeth Cady Stanton published the first volume of *The Woman's Bible*. She hoped that women would begin to question the theological ideas that so often cast them as inferior to men. Stanton also wondered why women were willing to challenge their places in their everyday lives but were not comfortable doing the same thing in the religious world. In her book, Stanton took verses from the Bible and analyzed them in terms of their significance for women, often reevaluating traditional interpretations.

The two volumes of *The Woman's Bible* were shocking to both women and men who believed that the Bible was the absolute word of God. Even some women in the suffrage movement objected to the book, believing that it hurt their cause. However, both volumes of *The Woman's Bible* became best sellers. The book was the very first seed of what would someday become feminist theology.

Some modern religions currently practiced in the United States have gained a reputation for restricting the roles of women in the church. Catholicism is one of the largest religions in the United States, with 24 percent of the religious population. However, it has continually refused women certain positions in the church. Islam is often pointed to as a religion that relegates women to a separate and not necessarily equal status in the mosque. Some Protestant churches also prohibit the ordination of women. The Reverend Betty Bone Schiess disagrees with religions that exclude women or relegate them to lesser roles. She believes these religions also affect society's attitudes about women. She wrote,

> The church influences society whether society acknowledges it or not. In fact, it has been suggested that no permanent social change takes place without a religious dimension. . . . When God, as interpreted by church action, says that women are the second order of creation, [women] are in real trouble.[2]

In 2008, according to the United States Department of Labor, women made up only 14.8 percent of all

Barbara Clementine Harris

On February 11, 1989, Barbara Clementine Harris became the first female bishop of the Episcopal Church. She became a deacon, and then a priest, before becoming an assisting bishop in the diocese, or district of churches, of Massachusetts. She was the first woman and the twenty-ninth African-American elected as a bishop. There was some controversy over her election. She had been divorced and her education and ministerial background were not standard. As a bishop, Harris has worked to make sure that the church does not ignore issues such as racism and sexism.

religious clergy. In Christian seminaries, women make up one third of the students. And yet, these women still struggle to be accepted as the equals of men in clerical roles. And it is only recently that the contributions women have made to their religions throughout history have even been studied.

The Heart of the Controversy

As society moves deeper into the twenty-first century, should women still be subject to the traditional restrictions on the religious roles they can have? Is it more important to a religion that women maintain their historical roles, for the good of the church and the future of their faith? Should women be given the same equality in every religion that they are gaining in society? Will religions survive without women to fill these leadership roles, especially in cases where men are entering the clergy in fewer numbers? All of these questions open the debate over what roles women should have in their religions. ⌒

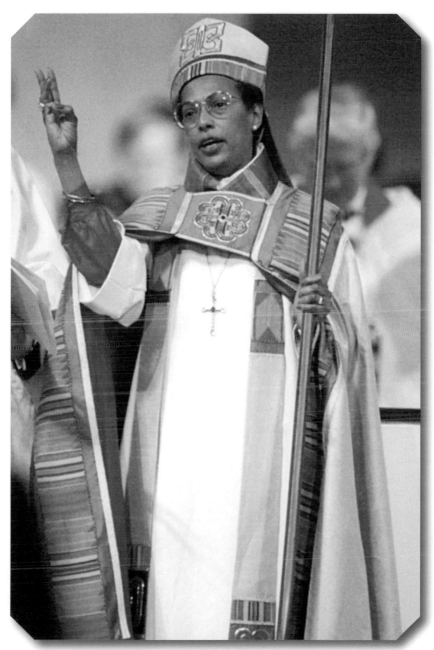

Barbara Clementine Harris was the first female bishop of
the Episcopal Church.

Chapter 2

Anne Hutchinson was banished from the Puritan Massachusetts Bay Colony.

BEFORE THE TWENTIETH CENTURY

In 1634, Anne Hutchinson and her family traveled from England to the Puritan colony located in what is now Massachusetts. Anne's husband, William, was a merchant, and Anne was an experienced midwife. Like the other Puritans, they were both devoutly religious. It would be Anne's duty as a Puritan wife and mother to help establish a religious household in this new world.

In addition to her other activities, Anne began holding weekly meetings to discuss the Bible and the sermon given the previous Sunday by the minister. At first, only women attended these meetings. But soon, Anne was holding a second weekly meeting that was attended by both men and women. Her views on religion were controversial because they did not always agree with those held by the church elders. Eventually, Anne was tried by the church for heresy. She was excommunicated and banished from the Massachusetts Bay Colony in 1637. Hugh Peters, one of the ministers at Anne's trial, said to her, "You have stept [sic] out of your place, you have rather [been] a Husband than a Wife and a preacher than a Hearer; and a Magistrate than a Subject."[1]

KEEPING TO THEIR PLACE

Anne Hutchinson's situation illustrates the role that women were expected to play in religion in early America. In one respect, Puritan women were equal to men when it came to spirituality. The most important role any person played in Puritan society was to believe in God. Women had to maintain a religious household and educate their children in the faith. They were expected to participate in their church, but only within the guidelines that had been established for them. According to Susan Hill Lindley, who wrote about Anne Hutchinson, "Women could be either good or bad, depending not only on their individual [devotion to a religious belief] . . . but also on their acceptance and fulfillment of particular social roles."[2]

Puritans also believed that women were naturally weaker and more likely to give in to temptation than men. Many women who were outspoken and did not obey the authority of their husbands or church leaders were often accused of witchcraft. If convicted, they were usually executed. Between 1620 and 1725, 344 people were accused of witchcraft in New England. Of those accused, 35 were executed, 28 of whom were female.

Ann Hibben

Women were often accused of witchcraft just because they happened to have strong personalities. In 1656, Ann Hibben of Boston, Massachusetts, was accused of witchcraft. The wife of a wealthy and prominent merchant, she had an unfortunate habit of getting into disputes with workmen. She had a reputation for being short-tempered and crabby. She was also accused of not being obedient to her husband. Hibben refused to accept the reprimand of her church or change her ways. The church excommunicated her. Later, she was accused, convicted, and hanged as a witch.

THE GREAT AWAKENING

As the first half of the eighteenth century unfolded, the American colonies were swept up in a series of religious movements known as the Great Awakening. Religious excitement spread as traveling ministers preached revival services. They focused on the importance of converting people to Christianity and declaring their belief in God. Instead of needing lengthy religious instruction, anyone could be converted and saved, no matter their social status. This had always been the case for Puritans, but now a greater emphasis was put on the personal conversion experience. This had the effect of making the individual more important than the church authorities. A person's status in society was now defined by whether or not he or she had a conversion experience.

Instead of the former style of a minister preaching to his congregation in a church setting, many revival ministers had more informal services where people—including women—were invited to speak in public about their conversion experiences or to encourage others to convert. Women were especially good at encouraging the men in their families to experience conversion.

Traveling ministers preached revival services during the Great Awakening.

The Great Awakening also spurred women to tackle many social issues. Women had long been considered the "backbone" of the church, doing much of the work behind the scenes. They taught Sunday school and supported missions and good works through women's circles. Soon, this role expanded even more. As Ann Braude explains in her book *Women and American Religion,*

> *The most important innovation for women . . . was the idea that it was not enough to experience conversion; conversion must be followed by a commitment to reform both one's personal habits and the society in which one lived.*[3]

This led to women's involvement in issues such as temperance, abolitionism, and, eventually, women's suffrage. Religious reform would teach women the skills they needed for these social reform movements.

MESSAGES FROM BEYOND

Spiritualism, which took hold in the mid-nineteenth century, was another religious movement that changed the way women were perceived in religion. Spiritualists believed that communicating with the spirits of dead people proved that the soul was immortal. Communication occurred during séances. At a séance, a medium served as the connection between the living and the dead. Women were said to be the best mediums. And because women were only saying what was being spoken "through" them as mediums, they could overcome the disapproval usually associated with women speaking in public during that time period. They were only the vehicles for the spirits' voices.

Spiritualism led to another religion that was founded by a woman. Mary Baker Eddy had experimented with Spiritualism. But she felt that the events taking place during séances were not due to spirits but, rather, the power of the human mind. In 1875, Eddy named her new religion Christian Science. She felt that the spirit was stronger than the body and that both the spirit and body could control physical matter. Christian Scientists believed all illness could be healed by the mind through an understanding of the Bible and God. Women were encouraged to explore the abilities of their minds. Christian Science also gave women

The Fox Sisters

As Spiritualism gained popularity in the United States, three of the biggest "stars" of the movement were sisters Ann Leah, Margaret, and Kate Fox. In 1848, they became the first spirit mediums in the nation. After Margaret and Kate heard mysterious rapping in the walls of their family farmhouse in New York, all three girls claimed to receive messages from the dead. As their fame spread, they began giving public demonstrations of communication with the spirit world and holding private séances all over the country. Although the Fox sisters contributed to the rise of Spiritualism as a religion, skepticism followed them throughout their lives.

the role model of a strong woman as the central figure of a religion.

GIFTS OF THE SPIRIT

At the beginning of the twentieth century, Pentecostal churches offered women even more opportunities for making their voices heard. Pentecostals believed that the Second Coming of Christ was about to happen. They believed that, during these last days of Earth, Christians could experience the gifts of the spirit described in

Jarena Lee

Jarena Lee is probably the first woman to become a preacher in the African Methodist Episcopal Church. Born in 1783, Lee was hired out as a servant at the age of seven. After having several conversion experiences in the early 1800s, she began to feel a call from God to go out and preach to others about her religion. However, she was told that women could not preach in the Methodist Church. Finally, in 1811, she began to actively pursue preaching. However, her minister soon discouraged her from this path.

Lee stopped trying to preach and got married. But after the death of her husband, Lee again felt the need to speak out about her faith. She began holding prayer meetings in her home. While she could not become a licensed minister with a congregation of her own, Lee finally received the support of her church to become an itinerant preacher in 1818. This allowed her to travel the eastern seaboard and give sermons to both black and white congregations. This was the only option for women who felt the call to preach during this time period.

Eventually, Lee published several books about her religious experiences. She sold the books at her meetings. Although little is known about her later life and date of death, Jarena Lee spent many years and traveled thousands of miles to share the gospel. She was one of the first women of her era to do so.

the Bible, such as the ability to heal and "speak in tongues." Speaking in tongues involved spontaneous outbursts, sometimes in unrecognizable languages. They occurred most often in women who then spoke so freely and for so long that Pentecostal ministers did not have time to deliver their sermons. Some women became leaders in Pentecostal churches due to their ability to speak in tongues.

As the United States moved further into the twentieth century, women assumed important and vital roles in many religions by speaking or working in missionary and aid groups to address social issues. However, they were still denied formal leadership roles. Women would continue to seek equality in the home, workplace, and society as a whole. ‿

Mary B. G. Eddy

Mary Baker Eddy founded the Christian Science Church in 1875.

Elizabeth Cady Stanton published The Woman's Bible *in 1895.*

LIBERATION AND CHANGING ROLES

I n 1895, Elizabeth Cady Stanton had her book *The Woman's Bible* published. Stanton was one of the leaders of the suffrage movement. She felt that organized religion had been harmful to women's rights:

It is not commendable for women to get up fairs and donation parties for churches in which [they] may neither pray, preach, share in the offices and honors, nor have a voice in the business affairs, creeds, and discipline, and from whose altars come forth Biblical interpretations in favor of women's subjection.[1]

In *The Woman's Bible*, Stanton reevaluated traditional interpretations of the Bible and how it represented women. And as women reached out for more and more equality, their position within the church continued to create controversy.

"Dangerously Feminized"

During the late nineteenth century, some U.S. church denominations were concerned about women's involvement in the church and its missions. There were more female than male members in most churches. Women carried out

Aimee Semple McPherson

In the 1920s, one of the most entertaining female religious leaders was Aimee Semple McPherson, the founder of the International Church of the Foursquare Gospel. She had a dramatic preaching style that she had learned by preaching in traveling tent revival meetings. Her church services were entertaining as well as inspirational. During her services, she usually wore a white dress and blue cape. From 1923 until 1926, McPherson preached to crowds of 5,000 every night at her Angelus Temple in Los Angeles. During one service, she arrived onstage on a motorcycle, dressed like a policeman, to give a dramatic sermon entitled "Stop! You're Under Arrest!" warning her audience that they were speeding down the wrong road in life.

most of the works of the churches, leading some men to worry that religion in the United States was "dangerously feminized."[2] Many churches broke up women-only missionary societies and combined them with their male counterparts to form more general church boards. This deprived women of one of their few sources of authority within the church.

WOMEN'S RIGHTS IN SOCIETY AND RELIGION

The twentieth century brought with it a growing interest in the rights of women. The suffrage movement and passage of the Nineteenth Amendment in 1920 secured women the right to vote.

Some denominations, such as the Protestant Unitarian and Congregationalist denominations, had ordained a few women since the nineteenth century. But ordination did not necessarily mean that these women would be installed as ministers of a church. In the 1930s, a Chicago Congregational Church advisory board wrote to one of its female seminary students,

> It is because we know so well the frustration awaiting any woman in the ministry that we are urging you to

enter related work. . . . There's only a slight chance you'd get a church and little promotion or professional advancement if you did.[3]

Despite these attitudes, some denominations began accepting women as ordained preachers. However, there were often restrictions. The Methodist Church allowed women to become local preachers in 1920, but they could not be full voting members of the denomination's ruling committees. By the 1950s, this started to change. During

---

The Church and the Second Sex

Born in 1928, Mary Daly grew up as a Catholic in Schenectady, New York. As an adult, she received advanced degrees in religion and philosophy. She hoped to achieve a doctorate in sacred theology from a Catholic faculty (the highest level of theological learning in the Catholic Church). However, she had to go outside the United States to find an authorized university willing to admit a woman.

Daly had observed the Vatican Council II, which addressed women's roles in the Catholic Church, but began to feel that women were being treated as second-class citizens in the Church. She recognized that there was a new era opening where women might achieve change within the Church.

In 1968, Daly published *The Church and the Second Sex*. The book argued that the Catholic Church was responsible for promoting women as inferior, even though the Church claimed that all humans were worthy of equal respect. The book was one of the most important written critiques of sexism in the Catholic Church.

After unsuccessfully trying to change the Catholic Church from within and dealing with the controversy over her book, Daly left the Church. She felt that the inferior status of women was too entangled in church doctrine to ever be changed. In later books, Daly has advocated starting new religions where women are central.

The opening ceremony during the third session of the Vatican Council II

World War II, many women had entered the work force while men were serving in the war. After the war, some women continued to seek employment opportunities. Churches were growing at this time and church leaders needed more preachers. So, the Methodist and Presbyterian churches began ordaining women with the same rights as their male equivalents. Pentecostal churches were especially likely to ordain women as religious leaders.

The strength of the civil rights movement in the 1960s led to a new women's movement. As previous movements had done, this movement called for equal opportunities for women in education, employment, and government offices. And, often through new legislation, women finally achieved these goals. Many women also rebelled against traditional roles for women as mothers and wives. As women started to achieve greater equality in the social and domestic spheres, some women began to demand more rights in their churches as well.

VATICAN COUNCIL II

In 1963, Pope John XXIII, head of the Catholic Church, assembled bishops from around the world to discuss changes to update the views of the Catholic Church. The pope noted,

Vatican Council II

The Vatican Council II was a special meeting held by the Roman Catholic Church. The council met in Rome for four separate sessions. The first session went from October 11 to December 8, 1962. In 1963, the second session began on September 29 and ended on December 4. The third session ran from September 14 to November 21, 1964. And, in 1965, the fourth and final session started September 14 and ended December 8. At the Vatican Council II, 2,500 bishops attended each session to discuss ways to reform the Roman Catholic Church. It was the first council of this kind since 1870.

Since women are becoming ever more conscious of their human dignity, they will not tolerate being treated as mere material instruments, but demand rights befitting a human person both in domestic and in public life.[4]

The group of bishops assembled to discuss the Church in the modern world publicly declared,

Every type of discrimination, whether social or cultural, whether based on sex, race, color, social condition, language or religion, is to be overcome and eradicated as contrary to God's intent.[5]

Despite these attempts to encourage women's roles in the Church, the only change was to admit women as observers to the Vatican Council II proceedings, but without the right to speak or vote. The Catholic Church still refused to allow women to become priests.

In 1994, Pope John Paul II announced,

I declare that the Church has no authority whatsoever to confer priestly ordination on women and that this judgment is to be definitively held by all the Church's faithful.[6]

Women who had hoped for more changes were disappointed, while others agreed with the pope's declaration. However, because of an increasing shortage of men wanting to become priests, Catholic canon laws changed to allow women to provide pastoral care as paid—but not ordained—pastoral leaders.

A SUCCESSFUL STRUGGLE

Women continued to reach for greater rights within their churches, and not every denomination refused them. As early as 1919, the Episcopal Church had discussed the question of ordaining women. They decided that as far as the beliefs of the church were concerned, there was no barrier to ordaining women, but neither was there a need for it. By 1970, women were allowed to become deacons, a step that usually led a man to being ordained as an Episcopal priest.

Women who were stalled in their position as ordained deacons waited for the Episcopal House of Bishops to approve women as priests. In 1974, a group of 11 women deacons held

Alla Bozarth-Campbell

Ordained as an Episcopal deacon in 1971, Alla Bozarth-Campbell was unable to become a priest. The church refused to allow women in that position. When her husband was ordained as a priest in 1974, she stood in the doorway at the back of the church and answered the same questions he was being asked by the presiding bishop. When the bishop and other priests laid hands on Bozarth-Campbell's husband, confirming him as a new priest, another deacon, one priest, and several women moved to the back of the church and laid their hands on her to show that she had every right to be a priest just as her husband now was.

Women-Church

In November 1983, a group of 1,400 women met in Chicago, Illinois, for a conference called "From Generation to Generation: Women Church Speaks." Most of these women were from the Catholic Church and had become disenchanted with organized religion. As a result of this conference, Women-Church was born. It is a national network of feminist communities and organizations that seeks to include women in all aspects of the church and support each other as they live their faith experience. Any women's group with three or more members can call itself a Women-Church. The association is not concerned with membership, growth, or a formal structure.

their own ordination without the approval of the church. Three retired bishops agreed to ordain them. In 1976, the Episcopal Church's general convention debated for four hours before voting to allow the ordination of women. Some members of the Episcopal religion left the church because of this decision. Some bishops still refuse to allow women priests to serve in their diocese.

PERSISTENT ARGUMENTS FOR TRADITIONAL ROLES

Although as many as half of all the religious groups in the United States ordain women, some religions have stepped back from allowing women to participate in church leadership. The arguments against ordaining women in Protestant churches usually center on the Bible and scriptures that seem to specifically point to men as the leaders of the church. The Bible states that God created man and then created woman to be his helper. This is often interpreted as meaning that the hierarchy of the church should be God, Christ, man, and then woman. Some proponents of traditional roles argue that because Eve, the first woman, was the one who gave into temptation first in the Garden of Eden, women are inferior and thus unfit to hold leadership positions in the church.

Many evangelical churches feel that the Bible prescribed traditional roles for women. These churches cite that in an increasingly lax society, it is important to adhere to those roles and keep church leadership strictly male. The Southern Baptist Church (SBC), which had previously ordained some women, voted to ban the practice in 1984. They believe that female ministers are in conflict with their interpretation of the Bible. The SBC convention issued the following pronouncement:

> *Explicit texts of scripture forbid women to serve as pastors. The biblical model for family roles supports that stance as well. It is not a matter of inferiority or worth, for all persons are of equal worth in their persons, reflecting the essential equality of the Godhead. It is a matter of function. There is*

*no compelling reason to encourage women as pastors, and
there are many reasons not to do so.*[7]

A WORLD OF CHOICE

In the twenty-first century, women face many
choices in their lives. This includes the ability to
pursue roles beyond the traditional scope as well as
the right to choose to follow those traditional gender
roles.

With these freedoms, some women have left
established religion in order to join alternative
religions that are based on female attributes or
goddess worship. Others have continued to fight
to be allowed to carry out the same leadership roles
as men in their particular church. And still more
choose to follow the traditional dictates of their
religion and the roles assigned to men and
women.

A woman prays at her church.

A bishop of the United Methodist Church celebrating communion

WOMEN AND PROTESTANTISM

*P*rotestantism is the largest movement within Christianity. It originated in the sixteenth century with the Protestant Reformation, when factions broke away from the Catholic Church. Like Catholics, Protestants believe in God and Jesus

Christ as his son. However, Protestants believe that the Bible is the final source of religious authority rather than church tradition or a religious authority, such as Catholicism's pope. Protestants also believe that people can find salvation through faith alone and not by performing good works.

Today, there are approximately 800 million Protestants worldwide. Protestantism includes many different denominations, such as Amish, Congregational, Lutheran, Mennonite, Methodist, Presbyterian, Quaker, and Shaker. Each group may worship in its own distinct way, hold its own specific religious beliefs, and view gender roles differently. Different denominations of Protestantism vary widely in their acceptance of women in the church.

PROTESTANT WOMEN LEADERS

The Congregational denomination, which became part of the United Church of Christ in 1931, has long been known for its

Fanny Crosby

Some of the most notable women in the Protestant religion never preached or stepped outside of their traditional roles. Fanny Crosby, who was born in 1820 and became blind as an infant, is the author of some of the best-known hymns in Protestant churches. Her hymns were tremendously popular and commercial successes. In her lifetime, Crosby wrote the words to approximately 9,000 hymns—many were written under pseudonyms. Songs such as "All the Way My Savior Leads Me," "Rescue the Perishing," and "Blessed Assurance" are still sung today.

tolerant attitudes and its support of equal human rights, including the rights of women. The first woman to be ordained as a minister in a Protestant denomination, Antoinette Brown Blackwell, was a Congregationalist. In 1853, she was ordained as a minister of a Congregational church in New York. Blackwell would lead the way for all women seeking to be ordained as members of the Protestant clergy and helped establish Protestant churches as some of the most open to women in leadership roles.

However, each Protestant church differs in its ideas of women's roles in the church. While groups such as the Episcopal Church, which decided to permit women to become priests, believe that women and men should be allowed to fulfill the same roles, other sects believe that women should occupy a traditional role.

Some denominations, such as the Pentecostal churches, started out with a large number of women leaders, but the number has decreased over the years. Sheri R. Benvenuti, a Pentecostal minister, witnessed this shift:

> Pentecostal women who are called to ministry walk a fine and often precarious line. We, on the one hand, are not radical

feminists. . . . However, on the other hand, we are not simply passive about our call to ministry.[1]

Benvenuti goes on to say that while the church continues to debate the role of women in its ministry, there is an increasing need for more anointed people to preach the gospel in the modern world.

ADVOCATING TRADITIONAL ROLES FOR WOMEN

Some Protestant denominations feel that women should not have a place in the leadership of a church. Many of these groups believe that men and women are designed by God to complement each other. According to these denominations, men are to provide for and protect their families. Women are to respect their husbands and serve as their helpers in maintaining the household and raising children.

Helen Barrett Montgomery

Born in 1861, Helen Barrett Montgomery is the first woman to be elected president of a major religious denomination. As a member of a Baptist church, she taught Bible classes and served as the president of a woman's union and the Women's American Baptist Foreign Mission Society. She held a license to preach from her congregation even though she was never ordained. Montgomery toured the world to get a firsthand impression of missionary work and wrote a book about her experiences. She also translated the Greek New Testament into modern English. In 1921, she was elected president of the Northern Baptist Convention.

Amish women are not allowed to be leaders in their churches.

As an extension of this belief, it is not appropriate for women to hold church leadership roles that involve teaching or holding authority over men.

One of the main advocates of this view is an evangelical organization called the Council on Biblical Manhood and Womanhood (CBMW). The council was established to address the impact of feminism on the church and on society in general.

The CBMW is concerned about the effect feminism could have on future generations:

> *The Bible clearly teaches that men and women are equal in value and dignity and have distinct and complementary roles in the home and the church. If churches disregard these teachings and accommodate to the culture, then the members of those churches and subsequent generations will be less likely to submit to God's word in other difficult matters as well.* [2]

Denominations that agree with these beliefs are afraid that if women are allowed leadership roles, the church and the family unit will be weakened permanently.

Amish & Mennonite: A Biblical Hierarchy

The Amish and the Mennonite are among the religious denominations that believe men and women's roles should be defined according to the Bible. These two groups are known for maintaining simple, unmodernized lifestyles. The Amish live without automobiles, electricity, and other modern technology. In Amish churches, the leadership is completely male. During Sunday worship services, men and women do not sit together. Amish women are not allowed to be leaders in their church.

The Mennonite Church has more variation within its membership. Some Mennonites believe that women should be nurturing, submissive, and godly, while men are leaders and providers. More progressive Mennonite communities allow women to pursue education and careers. Women may even hold positions as deacons or ministers in the church. But most Mennonites believe that the Biblical hierarchy of "God-Christ-man-woman" clearly places men above women and prevents women from holding leadership roles.

Protestant denominations such as the Amish and the Mennonite that advocate more traditional gender roles are thriving. According to author Ann Braude:

> Since the mid-1960s, the fastest growing religious groups in the United States have been those that take . . . conservative positions on women's role. Most of these emphasize homemaking and child rearing as God-given roles for women, do not ordain women, and view [women's lesser status than men] as mandated by the Bible. . . . In addition to the popularity of their beliefs, these groups are growing because of high birthrates, which they encourage.[3]

Mormons: Changing Roles

In the Mormon Church (the Church of Jesus Christ of Latter-Day Saints), women's roles within the church have changed since it was founded in 1830. Originally, women held more responsibility for nurturing the church and helping others. They were seen as having equal "gifts of the Spirit." Women often administered blessings, healed the sick, and prophesied future events. However, only men were allowed to carry out the more formal functions of ministry.

The Quakers

Of all the Protestant denominations, the Quaker religion has been more open to women throughout its history in the United States, even though it limited women's leadership roles during some periods. The Quaker church, also known as the Society of Friends, was founded in England in 1652. In 1656, the first Quakers arrived in North America. From its beginning, Quakers believed that the "inner light of Christ" existed in every person, and congregations should not have one formal pastoral authority. Instead, they preferred to have lay preachers, members of the congregation who were moved by the spirit to speak. Those who spoke during a meeting were usually formally recognized as ministers. This included a large number of women. Quakers also held separate, equal meetings for men and women. This gave women the opportunity to learn organizational skills and to speak out on social issues.

Quaker women became very influential in nineteenth-century U.S. reform movements, such as abolitionism and suffrage. Some historians feel that the values of the Quaker religion, such as nonviolent protest and the inclusion of women from all races and classes, are a result of so many Quaker women being involved in these reform movements.

As the church grew and the practice of multiple marriages was introduced, women's roles in the church became limited. In the 1970s, the Mormon Church opposed the Equal Rights Amendment that advocated for equal rights for men and women, and the church excommunicated several women who supported it. Some Mormons look at the history of their church and wonder why women had greater freedom and more leadership positions at one time. Some wish to return to the freedoms of those times. Others are satisfied with their position in the church. Meanwhile, the church continues to endorse the idea that women should be solely homemakers, wives, and mothers.

A Variety of Choices

Even though Protestant denominations are united by a belief in the Bible and the role of the individual in his or her own salvation, they vary widely in the acceptable roles and expectations for women. However, compared with women in religions such as the Catholic Church, Protestant women generally have more leadership opportunities.

A Mennonite woman makes dinner for her family. In most cases, Mennonites advocate for traditional gender roles.

Pope Benedict XVI became head of the Catholic Church in 2006.

WOMEN AND CATHOLICISM

Roman Catholics are the largest group of Christians in the world. More than 1 billion people belong to that faith. In the United States alone, there are more than 67 million Catholics, making up approximately 22 percent of the U.S. population. Catholics and Protestants hold similar beliefs in God and Jesus Christ as his son, but the pope is the ultimate authority in the Catholic religion. He is believed to be infallible, meaning that his declarations on matters of faith and morals are without error and must be followed by all Catholics. The Catholic Church maintains very specific moral teachings. It condemns the use of artificial birth control, abortion, and some current medical practices related to fertility, such as in vitro fertilization, surrogate pregnancies, and artificial insemination. The Catholic Church has also maintained a firm stand against ordaining women as priests.

Because the Catholic Church and the pope have made specific pronouncements concerning issues that affect women, Catholic women have to make some serious choices. Will they follow the rules of their faith exactly as they are specified or risk violating those rules for the sake of their personal lifestyle and family choices?

A Woman's Church

Even though the Catholic Church appears to be dominated by males, it is also rich in female role models. The Virgin Mary (the mother of Jesus Christ) is one of the most honored women in the religion. She is exalted for her role as the mother of the son of God. She can be called on by women and men to intercede with Jesus for help.

The Catholic Church also has a large number of female saints. Throughout history, women have been canonized because of their deeds or conduct. Some have lost their lives because they refused to act against their faith. Others are saints because of their contributions to the Church.

The Catholic Church also has many religious orders for women. There are two different types of roles that women can have within religious orders. Nuns live within a cloistered environment. They take vows of poverty, celibacy, and obedience, spending their lives in prayer and meditation. Sisters belong to active religious orders with simpler vows. They play a larger role within the church ministry and their surrounding communities. These orders are often involved in teaching, nursing, and caring for the poor.

Nuns and sisters used to wear religious habits comprised of long gowns and complete head coverings. However, as a result of the changes made

A stained glass image of the Virgin Mary holding Jesus

by Vatican II, many began modifying their dress,
with the reasoning that formal habits made it more
difficult to establish communication with people
in the communities they were serving. Regardless
of which type of order these women belong to, they
accomplish some of the most important work of
their church.

However, the number of women entering
religious orders has been steadily declining. In 1945,
more than 122,000 women lived in religious orders.

By 2008, that number had decreased to less than 60,000. A parallel exists between the opportunities available for women in a society and the decline of religious orders in that same society. Modern women often find careers more appealing than religious life.

Split Views

Some Catholics are critical of the male-dominated church governance that keeps women in specific roles as wives, mothers, and caregivers. The Church relies on women to carry out certain administrative roles within the Church. However, it refuses to allow women to become priests or to use medical forms of birth control.

Other Catholics rally behind their church's teachings. The Women for Faith and the Family organization (WFF), founded in 1984, is made up of Catholic women who support the conservative teachings of their church. The group helps women deepen their understanding of their faith and receive support from other women with similar beliefs. The WFF

Little Sisters of Jesus

One group of Catholic sisters has found a unique way to serve others and spread the message of their faith. The Little Sisters of Jesus believe that, rather than leading a contemplative life in a cloister, they belong out in the world, working and living among real people in real conditions. They are especially called to work in low-paying jobs, side by side with poor people, where they believe they can do the most good.

also makes statements about issues that affect women and the Church. These include feminism, the role of women in Catholicism, and current events with moral or religious implications.

THE CATHOLIC CHURCH AND BIRTH CONTROL

Some of the firmest-held beliefs of the Catholic Church seem to affect women the most. In 1968, Pope Paul VI wrote a landmark letter called *Humanae Vitae* ("Human Life") in which he emphasized the Catholic Church's teaching that any form of birth control was wrong. In the eyes of the Church, the purpose of marriage is procreation. It is wrong to prevent the birth of children, either through contraception, sterilization, or abortion. The Catholic Catechism states,

> *Human life is sacred because from its very beginning it involves the creative action of God . . . . God alone is the Lord of life from its beginning until its end: no one can under any circumstance claim for himself the right directly to destroy an innocent human being.*[1]

The Catholic Church does allow natural family planning methods. However, these are generally less effective than medical forms of birth control. As a result, devout Catholic women may have multiple pregnancies and large families. Or they may choose to control the size of their families with medical birth control methods, which violate the teachings of their church.

The Women Priests Controversy

Other than reproductive rights, the biggest issue affecting women in the Catholic Church is whether they should be allowed to become priests. Women today are carrying out many different roles within the Church, including that of pastoral administrator.

As pastoral administrators, women can perform most of the duties of priests, including overseeing church

Elizabeth Ann Seton

Elizabeth Ann Seton, also known as Mother Seton, was the founder of the Sisters of Charity. This Catholic sisterhood was dedicated to education, health, and helping seniors, sick people, and orphaned children. Mother Seton was also the first person born in the United States to be canonized into sainthood by the Catholic Church. Widowed at an early age with young children to raise, she supported herself by running a boardinghouse.

After converting to the Catholic religion, she opened a small school and formed the Sisters of Charity. She took her vows as a sister of the Catholic Church in 1809. She was able to run her religious order on very little money.

Mother Seton died in 1821 from tuberculosis. In 1975, she was canonized as Saint Elizabeth Ann Seton in recognition of her contributions to the Catholic Church and several miraculous cures that resulted from her work.

finances, visiting the sick, delivering homilies, and saying prayers. They cannot, however, lead any sacramental rituals, such as anointing of the sick. Most of their duties are also limited to the local level as well. As one Catholic woman commented,

> There are women who work at the United States Catholic Conference. . . . They might run an office there, the office of the laity, or something like that. But actually very few women do those things at the national level. I mean, it's really the Old Boy's Club that makes the decisions there in the Vatican.[2]

Some Catholic women are forming groups to encourage the Catholic Church to ordain women as priests. One such organization is the Roman Catholic Womenpriests (RCWP). The RCWP rejects the pope's ruling on female priests and has been ordaining women since 2002. The group advocates for the equality of sexes within the Catholic Church.

However, the Catholic Church does not agree with the Womenpriests and others who support the ordination of women. The Vatican declared that any women who try to become priests or men who assist them will be excommunicated from the Church. The Catholic Church believes that only a man can receive a call from God to become a priest. As priest, he is meant to represent Jesus Christ himself, so he must be male like Christ. Additionally, Catholics advocating this belief point to the fact that Christ chose only male apostles. They assert that if Christ had wanted women to be religious leaders, he would have picked female apostles.

In the early 2000s, due to a declining number of men entering the priesthood, there were no longer enough priests to serve all Catholic churches. In 2002, approximately 15 percent of Catholic parishes did not have their own priests. Some people pointed to these numbers as reasons why it is important to ordain women as priests. However, in 2009, a change occurred in the Catholic Church. On October 20, 2009, the Vatican announced that it would make it easier for Anglicans who were unhappy with their church to join the Catholic Church. Some Anglicans were upset when their church allowed women to become priests in the 1990s and bishops in 2008. Many were also upset when the church allowed homosexual clergy. Proponents of female Catholic priests worry that the influx of Anglican priests into the Catholic Church will fill the void in the priesthood and make it less likely for the Church to allow the ordination of women.

Women from the Roman Catholic Womenpriests ordain
women in their own ceremonies.

Orthodox Jewish women wait outside a synagogue in New York City in 2006.

WOMEN AND JUDAISM

The Jewish faith is thought to be the oldest monotheistic religion in the world. A monotheistic religion believes there is only one god who created the world and rules over it. Traditionally, Judaism has also been a religion with strict rules for conducting everyday life. These include clearly defined roles for men and women. Among other things, these rules specify what rituals are to be carried out, what people should wear, how they should worship, and what foods they can and cannot eat. A specific set of rules, called the *mitzvoth*, controls relationships between husbands and wives as well as parents and children.

Despite beliefs that unify them, members of the Jewish community have had disagreements over time as to how best to worship and live as Jews. As a result of these disagreements, several distinct divisions have come to exist in the Jewish religion. Depending on what division, or sect, of Judaism women follow, and how closely they adhere to that division's teachings, their roles may be limited.

ORTHODOX JUDAISM: TRADITIONAL ROLES

Orthodox Jews adhere most closely to the traditions of Judaism. Orthodox Jews believe that they practice the most traditional form of Judaism. They strive to follow the 613 commandments of the Jewish faith. Some Orthodox Jews live in modern society while still following many rules of their faith. Others, such as the Hasidic Jews, usually live apart in their own closely knit communities. They tend to have limited interaction with those outside their communities. Women in the Hasidic tradition rarely have careers and usually focus on being wives and mothers. They are not allowed to show their legs, necks, or elbows in public. Married women must keep their hair covered at all times. Even after marriage, men and women have very little social contact with each other in public.

Some people believe that Orthodox Judaism places unfair limitations on women. The Jewish Orthodox Feminist Alliance (JOFA) works to expand women's roles within the religion. This group believes that Orthodox Jewish women can stay true to their faith while increasing their leadership and participation within their religion. Some Orthodox congregations have begun allowing women to serve as rabbinical assistants, a role that involves teaching, counseling, visitations, and sometimes even preaching.

Allison Josephs is a writer who challenges public stereotypes of Orthodox Jews. She was raised as a Conservative Jew but converted to Orthodox Judaism after high school. She explained,

I was initially wary of Orthodox Judaism and its treatment of women. I was raised to believe, as many people are, that women are subjugated, second-class citizens in Orthodox society. But then I started meeting [Orthodox] Jews and my experiences were vastly different than the rumors I had grown up with.[1]

Other women who are practicing Orthodox Jews embrace the traditional roles given to them. They feel valued for their contributions in these roles that have been in place for thousands of years. According to Hasia Diner in *Her Works Praise Her*, "The

Blu Greenberg

As a young woman, Blu Greenberg grew up in an Orthodox Jewish home and received an excellent education. During her junior year in college in the late 1950s, she studied the Bible with a noted Biblical scholar in Israel. However, when she tried to extend her studies there, her family disapproved. Greenberg knew that if she had been male, the request would have been met differently. However, she did not agree with the more radical practices of feminism.

Greenberg continued to be troubled by the gender inequality in the Jewish faith. She is now a writer specializing in modern Orthodox Judaism and women's issues. She is actively involved in the movement to bridge the gap between Orthodox Jewish practice and feminism. She chairs international conferences on feminism and orthodoxy, helped set up a Women of Faith group for women of different faiths to interact, and launched the Dialogue Project, which unites Jewish and Palestinian women. She lectures to universities and community groups all over the country and has written several books, including *On Women and Judaism*. In 2000, she received the Women Who Made a Difference award from the American Jewish Congress Commission for Women's Equality.

sacred work of wife and mother . . . retain in many of today's Orthodox communities the same high esteem and deep richness that glorified them in the [past]."[2]

Bat Mitzvah

Before 1920, only young Jewish boys had a special ceremony, called a bar mitzvah, to celebrate their transition into adulthood. In 1922, Rabbi Mordecai Kaplan, the founder of Reconstructionism, felt that his daughter Judith deserved the same synagogue honors that a boy of her age and learning would get.

Today, many Jewish girls in the Reform and Conservative traditions celebrate a bat mitzvah when they reach the age of 12. This often includes reading from the Torah in Hebrew, during part of the religious service, which is followed by a celebratory meal and the giving of gifts. However, some Orthodox Jews do not have a ritual to celebrate the bat mitzvah or a coming of age ceremony for girls at all.

REFORM AND CONSERVATIVE JUDAISM: MORE LEADERSHIP

Reform Judaism, which is also called progressive or liberal Judaism, does not believe that the traditional rules of their religion must be followed exactly. Rather, Reform Jews focus on ethics and believe that the rules were written by men with God's help, and following God's will is a life-long process. Reform Jewish congregations were the first to allow women to be ordained as rabbis.

Conservative Judaism falls between the Orthodox and Reform traditions. Conservative Jews follow most of the traditional rules and practices of their faith. They initially opposed allowing women greater participation in the community.

A young girl reading from the Torah during her bat mitzvah

However, they have begun to allow women into roles
that previously were for males only. This includes
the rabbinate. A branch of Conservative Judaism
known as the Reconstructionist Movement has been
the most supportive of women's rights. It has created
ceremonies specifically addressing coming of age for
girls (known as bat mitzvahs), where previously only
boys had these ceremonies (bar mitzvahs).

These more reformed sects of Judaism have
allowed women more participation, especially in
worship. In 1972, Sally Jane Priesand was ordained

Paula Ackerman

As the wife of a rabbi of a Reform congregation, Paula Ackerman led the children's temple and filled in for her husband, William, when he traveled. In 1950, William Ackerman died. From January 1951 to the fall of 1953, until a male rabbi was selected, Paula became the rabbi of the Jewish congregation in Mississippi. She performed all the duties of a regular rabbi, including preacher, counselor, teacher, and manager of her congregation. The state of Mississippi gave her permission to perform marriages. She was the first woman to perform the functions of a rabbi.

as the first U.S. female rabbi by the Reform branch of Judaism. While she had difficulty finding a job initially, Priesand eventually became a rabbi with her own synagogue congregation at Monmouth Reform Temple in 1981. She also wrote a book about the limitations that Judaism places on women. Since she was ordained, nearly 1,000 women have become rabbis. Today, women in Reform Judaism are encouraged to become rabbis. This branch of Judaism has been foremost in taking previously male-only rituals and adapting them to mark events in women's lives. However, the Conservative Jewish movement did follow, ordaining its first female rabbi in 1985.

HADASSAH: A TRADITION OF STRONG WOMEN

Even though the different divisions of Judaism may have differing views of the appropriate role of women, all Jewish women have strong role models from the Bible, such as Miriam, Esther, and Deborah. Queen Esther, whose birth name was *Hadassah*, saved Israel from destruction because of her courage. In 1912, her name was given to what is now the largest Jewish women's organization in the world—Hadassah, the Women's Zionist Organization of America. Hadassah has helped establish medical facilities in Israel, helped relocate Jewish refugee children from places such as Nazi Germany and Ethiopia, and supports various education programs. Hadassah is committed to strengthening Jewish values and traditions throughout the world.

Hadassah also gave Jewish women a way to make a meaningful contribution to their faith. According to Henrietta Szold, who founded Hadassah after a trip to Palestine in 1910, "There is no more serious charge made against Judaism than the charge that women are neglected."[3]

The Miriam Cup

For thousands of years, the Jewish people have celebrated the annual Passover Seder meal. It commemorates the meal that the Jews hurriedly ate before fleeing from Egypt. At a traditional Seder meal, an extra cup is set on the table for the prophet Elijah. Recently, however, Jewish households have been including another cup—the Miriam cup. It recognizes that, according to the Bible, the prophetess Miriam, who was Moses's sister, helped Moses lead the Jews out of Egypt. It acknowledges the contributions made to the faith by generations of Jewish women. Miriam's cup is filled with water, to symbolize the miracle of Miriam's well in the desert, which kept the Jews alive on their long journey out of Egypt.

A Continuing Conflict

The differing beliefs about the roles that Jewish women should play within their places of worship and their faith continue. As with any modern religion within the United States, women in the Jewish faith can make choices according to how they worship and follow their faith. While the most traditional forms of Judaism limit what a woman can do, some women find these strict rules to be comforting and supportive. Others have left the more rigid forms of Judaism to pursue careers and larger roles. And some have been able to reconcile both careers and traditional rules in a way that they find satisfying. For the most part, Judaism allows women in the United States to choose their roles without fear of censure or violence, something that is not necessarily true for women in other religions.

Hillary Rodham Clinton gives a speech at the national convention of Hadassah.

Muslim women holding the Qur'an

WOMEN AND ISLAM

Approximately 1 billion people worldwide practice the religion of Islam. It is based on the teachings of the prophet Muhammad, who received the word of God (or Allah, in Arabic) more than 1,400 years ago at Mecca, which is located in what is now Saudi Arabia. Like Christianity, Islam believes in one creator, God. But Islam is a way of life as much as it is a religion. In Islam, there are no distinctions between the sacred and secular parts of everyday life. Islam's holy book, the Qur'an, contains the beliefs of Islam and the religious practices that Muslims everywhere must follow. The Five Pillars of Islam are the five essential practices that Muslims must perform. These include a declaration of faith, daily prayers, charitable giving, fasting during the holy month of Ramadan, and making a pilgrimage to Mecca at least once during one's life. However, there are great ranges in the practice of Islam in the United States and worldwide.

ISLAMIC COUNTRIES AND HUMAN RIGHTS

Many people in the Middle East and South and Southeast Asia are practicing Muslims. In some Islamic countries of the Middle East, such as Iran and Saudi Arabia, Islamic law is the same as the government law. Unlike the United States, there is no separation between the church and the government. Women hold a lesser status in society than men. Women may be married at very young ages to men much older than they are. According to Islamic law, Muslim men are allowed to have up to four wives at a time. Women in Islamic countries may also face difficulties if they try to divorce their husbands, even abusive ones.

Muslim women are also expected to be chaste and modest. Some Muslim communities practice female circumcision, which involves cutting a female's external sex organs. This is thought to reduce a women's sexual desire and keep a woman chaste. Especially in Islamic countries, some Muslims go to

Guilty of Going to School

In Kandahar, in southern Afghanistan, 15 girls and teachers were splashed with acid on their way to school in November 2008. This area has a large Taliban presence. The Taliban, which is a radical Islamic political group, has imposed a complete ban on any form of education for females. Men on a motorcycle approached the young women, who were wearing school uniforms and veils, and threw car battery acid on their faces.

great lengths to discourage what they see as dishonorable behavior. Muslim women can dishonor their families by marrying against their family's wishes or committing adultery. In some cases, Muslim women have been murdered when they have dishonored their family in this way. This is called an honor killing. It is believed that honor killings are actually cultural practices that predate Islam and were later incorporated into the religion. In the United States, honor killings are considered murders. But in many Islamic countries the killers are not punished. The disgrace the woman has brought on her family and herself by her actions is seen as enough reason to end her life.

Human rights groups are appalled by this treatment of women. For example, the Coalition for Sexual and Bodily Rights in Muslim Societies seeks to create laws against practices such as female circumcision and other forms of violence against women and girls.

Others argue that with these strict punishments come benefits for Muslim women. For example, Saudi Arabia is one of the most fundamentalist Islamic nations. There, women are required to veil themselves completely in a burka. In "Shattering Illusions: Western Conceptions of Muslim Women," Saimah Ashraf writes,

> [Women in Saudi Arabia] are not allowed to sit in the front seat of a car or walk alongside a man if he is not her husband or close relative; nor are women allowed to drive.[1]

Advocates of this treatment note that these women also receive privileges that other Muslim women may not, such as protection by their families and government, high dowries for marriage, and the right to keep their own wealth.

Interpreting the Qur'an

As with any religious scripture, multiple interpretations of the Qur'an have formed over time. For example, parts of the Qur'an have been interpreted to mean that men are meant to supervise and control women. One verse in the Qur'an explains that a husband who has a disobedient wife should give her a warning and let her sleep alone. If neither of these tactics make a difference in her behavior, the husband may beat his wife.

However, many Muslims believe that all humans are equal in the eyes of God. They do not interpret the Qur'an to condone honor killings, female circumcision, or a lesser status of women in society. The Muslim Women's League calls Muslims to "reject this distortion of Islam that is used to violate the most basic rights of human decency, integrity and justice."[2] According to Tasleem Griffin in the article "Within the Sheltering Peace: Islam and Women":

> *Not one verse in the whole of the Qur'an speaks injustice. Not one word says, men and women are not equal. . . . In a time when most women were common [property], the teachings of the Qur'an and the practices of Muhammad . . . firmly*

restored to them status, both legal and social; and dignity as individuals; cemented their right to wealth and property, to inheritance, to education.[3]

Burkas and Hijabs

In most Muslim communities in the United States, women may choose whether to wear a hijab, a scarf covering their hair, or a burka, which covers a woman from head to toe with only the eyes visible. In other countries, a woman does not have the opportunity to choose.

Naheed Mustafa is a young, university-educated Muslim woman living in Canada. She has chosen to wear the traditional hijab, which covers her head, neck, and throat for modesty. Mustafa finds that wearing the scarf brings many reactions from people around her, but she feels that wearing the hijab is beneficial:

> [W]earing the hijab has given me the freedom from constant attention to my

Practicing Islam

As with any religion, not all Muslim women practice their faith in the same way. Muslims in the United States are very diverse. Some practice their faith at home and do not attend a mosque; others are strictly traditional and observe Islamic law as closely as possible. Muslim women in the United States are more likely to attend a mosque than women in Islamic countries. Many perform open social roles such as fundraising, teaching, and organizing social activities.

physical self. . . . True equality will be had only when women don't need to display themselves to get attention.[4]

Hinduism

Although there are some Muslims in South Asia, most people there practice Hinduism. India, in particular, has a strong majority of Hindus. Hinduism places a strong emphasis on female divinity. Yet it is usually repressive when it comes to women's roles.

Hindus believe not only in one central god, but also in many other gods and goddesses who are seen as other forms or aspects of that god. Hindus place greater emphasis on the female aspects of the central god. Goddesses such as Kali, Durga, Lakshmi, and Sarasvati all represent different feminine qualities of the divine being.

Hindu women are traditionally seen as having only one duty in the world: to depend upon and be obedient to their husbands. This is especially true in cultures where women have not yet achieved a more equal social status. Traditionally, a Hindu woman has four roles in life: her husband's servant, a minister in his decision-making, the mother of his children, and his lover. She lives her life making vows to protect her husband and bring him prosperity. She is responsible for keeping her husband well and may be blamed for his death. Modern Hindu women often enjoy political equality with men. However, in parts of the world, many Hindu women suffer from discrimination as well as abuse, inheritance and dowry issues, and harassment.

Women in modern Western society who choose to wear hijabs as a way to express their religion often find themselves discriminated against. In the United States, Muslims are sometimes viewed with suspicion due to uninformed opinions about Islam. Women may have their hijabs ripped off or spit on. Some women may be fired from their jobs because their scarves conflict with their employer's dress codes. One such case went to court in 2009, when a Muslim woman working as a corrections officer in New Jersey was fired for insisting on wearing her headscarf at work. Muslim women wearing hijabs or burkas may even find themselves objects of pity because others consider the headscarf a sign of female oppression. As Sherif Abdel Azim, a professor at Queens University in Canada, comments,

> It is one of the great ironies of our world today that the very same headscarf revered as a sign of "holiness" when worn by Catholic nuns, is reviled as a sign of "oppression" when worn for the purpose of modesty and protection by Muslim women.[5]

WOMEN AS IMAMS

Certain sects of Islam, such as the Shiites, have spiritual leaders called imams who have authority over their congregations. Imams often lead worshippers in prayer. In most cases, women are not permitted to act as imams, except for an exclusively female group or a congregation consisting of only close relatives. Men and women are separated during prayer, sometimes in different rooms. Muslims continue to debate whether women should be allowed to lead public prayers and pray in front of a mixed-gender group.

In many American-Islamic congregations, imams are also expected to draw up marriage contracts, provide counseling, mediate judicial divorces, and teach adults and children. Many Muslim women feel that these imams could benefit from the availability of a female scholar or social worker to help deal with family conflicts and issues related specifically to women.

Freedom of Choice?

Although the United States guarantees freedom of religion, Muslim women do not always have access to these freedoms without compromising their faith or separating themselves from family or community. In the United States, legal protections and safe houses are available for Muslim women threatened with honor killings or beatings. However, women in other nations, especially Saudi Arabia and Pakistan, are more likely to be left without protection from punishment. ⌐

Sama Wareh of Newport Beach, California, wears special swimwear made for Muslim women.

Followers of the Wicca religion participate in a ritual at the Witch School in Hoopeston, Illinois.

WOMEN AND
ALTERNATIVE RELIGIONS

W hen it comes to defining their roles within the constraints of organized religions, some women in the United States have chosen to break away entirely from established spiritual groups. Many of these women have forged their own new religions, which are often centered entirely upon women.

Some women believe that traditional organized religions do not provide acceptable roles for them or that those religions' sets of beliefs diminish a woman's importance. Others are bothered by the use of masculine language and imagery in most religions. According to writer Ann Braude, "The goal of women's spirituality is to recover a connection among women, nature, and divine power believed to have been repressed during centuries of male-dominated religion."[1] For women who are seeking a different form of spiritually, alternative religions and neopaganism have provided another type of religious expression.

Neopaganism is the overall term for religions that attempt to revitalize ancient nature religions. These include Wicca, Druidism, and the worship of groups such as ancient Norse or Egyptian gods and goddesses. Many of these neopagan religions do not have established organizations or hierarchies, since their adherents feel that those are the types of restrictions that have hurt women's religious participation in the past.

A Wiccan Woman

Margot Adler was raised in a nonreligious family. Fascinated by Greek gods and goddesses at an early age, Adler became interested in paganism. She also disagreed with the traditional religious belief that man was meant to dominate Earth. Adler was drawn to pagan religions that viewed humans as an equal part of nature. In 1973, she began practicing the Wiccan religion, and in 1976, she became a neopaganist priestess. She later published several books and became a correspondent for National Public Radio.

Young Women and Wicca

Many of the women who convert to the Wiccan religion are young. Because the religion is centered around women and elevates them, it is especially appealing to younger women who may be rejecting the patriarchal religions they were brought up with. Wicca is also concerned with the environment and caring for Earth as well as being attuned to the cycles of nature, which also appeals to younger generations who have been raised with a greater awareness of these environmental concerns. Wicca has also received more positive mainstream publicity in recent years. Television shows such as *Sabrina, Buffy the Vampire Slayer,* and *Charmed,* as well as the movies *The Craft* and *Practical Magic,* bring neopagan religions and witchcraft into mainstream culture and often feature teenage characters.

Teens are occasionally attracted to Wicca because it serves as an alternative to traditional religions with restrictive moral beliefs, particularly about sex before marriage. Although followers are difficult to quantify because Wicca is not institutionalized, it appears that the number of young people involved in Wicca is growing.

Because Adler feels that the term "witch" has a
negative connotation for many people, she prefers to
be called a pagan. In response to those who consider
practitioners of witchcraft and the Wiccan religion to
be evil, she says:

> *We are not evil. We don't harm or seduce people. We are*
> *not dangerous. We are ordinary people like you. We have*
> *families, jobs, hopes, and dreams. We are not a cult. . . . You*
> *don't have to be afraid of us. We don't want to convert you.*
> *And please don't try to convert us. Just give us the same right*
> *we give you—to live in peace.* [2]

COMMON THEMES

Neopagan and alternative religions for women
have several common themes. Most involve
worshipping a female "goddess" deity, a mother,
or other female version of the divine. This goddess
figure affirms the powers of women—including
creativity, strength, and sexuality—which have been
repressed in traditional male-dominated religions.
As Carol P. Christ explains in her article "Why
Women Need the Goddess,"

> *Religion centered on the worship of a male God creates*
> *"moods" and "motivations" that keep women in a state of*

*psychological dependence on men and male authority, while
at the same time legitimating the political and social authority
of fathers and sons in the institutions of society.*[3]

These goddess-oriented religions also emphasize
worship rituals and communities that are led by
women. Some neopagan groups have gods as well as
goddesses and include both men and women. Others
remain solely feminine.

Many of these religions also have a close tie to
nature and emphasize how humans fit into all of
nature instead of focusing on achieving a divine
afterlife. These religions relate the goddess figure to
Mother Nature and environmental concerns. Most
neopagan religions focus on the individual and the
personal experience of spirituality instead of a set of
standardized rules and a formal structure.

Criticisms

Unlike traditional religions such as Catholicism,
Judaism, or Islam, neopagan religions such as
Wicca hold unlimited possibilities for women's
participation in private spirituality and leadership
of public worship rituals. However, some who
practice their faith through traditional religions

view goddess-centered neopagan religions as simply reversing sexism from men to women. They argue that these religions exclude men just as traditional religions exclude women. Some critics also argue that new religions based on societies that worshipped goddesses are not historically accurate. They believe that, in many cases, these ancient civilizations used goddesses as a way to emphasize the power of a male ruler. There are also debates about the value of a religion that emphasizes personal spiritual fulfillment without stressing the good of the community as well. The Wiccan religion maintains a basic moral principle (called a rede) that says "if it harms none, do as you will." According to James Lewis, author of *Witchcraft Today*, "Some feel that this is too slender a 'rede' on which to base an ethic adequate for a religious movement as large as Neopaganism."[4]

Starhawk

One of the best-known spokespersons for Wicca is Starhawk. She was born into a Jewish household, but during her college years she learned witchcraft. She later became one of the first women to sign the Covenant of the Goddess, a national Wiccan association. She founded Reclaiming: A Center for Feminist Spirituality and Counseling in Berkeley, California. The center offers classes, workshops, rituals, and counseling in witchcraft. She has written many books about Wicca and neopaganism. Starhawk has also increased contact between men and feminist women involved in neopagan religions by including men in many of her Wiccan rituals.

Many conservative Christians and other groups believe neopagan religions are a form of devil worship. However, neopaganists are quick to dismiss this claim. Wiccans explain that they do not believe in any evil entity, including Satan. Still, some Christians believe that neopaganists may unknowingly worship the devil.

Despite the arguments against neopagan, goddess-oriented religions, many women find them to be the only alternative to traditional religions and their restrictions on women. As Carol P. Christ says about a goddess-centered religion,

> *A woman is encouraged to know her will, to believe that her will is valid, and to believe that her will can be achieved in the world, three powers traditionally denied her in patriarchy.*[5]

EVERYTHING OLD IS NEW

It is not accurate, however, to say that every "new" religion is goddess-centered or neopagan. There are

Selena Fox

Selena Fox is a leader in the pagan-Wiccan community and founded the Circle Sanctuary in 1974, a Wiccan church in Wisconsin. Fox has been trained in a variety of disciplines, including alchemy, Native-American Shamanism, Druidism, Buddhism, and Christianity.

The Circle Sanctuary offers training to priestesses and priests in different pagan religions. Fox is also an advocate for religious freedom, campaigning for the rights of pagans to worship and to act as clergy in prisons. She also worked to defeat the Helms Amendment in 1985, which would have eliminated tax-exempt status for Wiccan churches.

still many religions developing that have returned
to traditional roles and practices for women, and
which some women willingly follow. One example is
the Messianic Community in Island Pond, Vermont
(formerly known as the Northeast Kingdom
Community Church). The Messianic Community
has roots in both Judaism and Christianity.
Members of this community live communally in
houses of three to eight families and work in church-
owned businesses.

Women in the Messianic Community are
required to wear headscarves as a symbol of their
submission to their husbands and the church elders.
They are not allowed to preach at religious services.
And yet, followers believe that the women actually
have greater authority in the church because of this.
As one male church leader explained:

> We believe in reconstructing relations between the sexes. By
> wearing a head scarf, the woman is showing she recognizes
> her rightful place. The world has been torn apart by the
> struggle between men and women. Once she stops fighting
> for power and stops manipulating and being greedy, then she
> is free to become really powerful. Women in our community
> have revelations; they can be prophetesses . . . We listen to

women who have wisdom. But authority works in a different way through women.[6]

The Messianic Community is only one example of religious communities that follow traditional gender roles. There is a trend toward returning to these roles for women as a response to more radically feminized religious roles in standard religions.

Be it a neopagan religion focused on women or a new version of a traditional religion, women are turning to alternative religious practices in greater numbers. Women in the United States are seeking their religious positions in many different churches and through many different roles.

Selena Fox founded a Wiccan church in Wisconsin.

*A member of the Women's Ordination Conference
protests in Lexington, Kentucky.*

THE FUTURE OF
WOMEN'S ROLES

The roles that women can and should play in religion remain a controversy that may never be fully resolved. Religion is a personal issue that extends beyond political and cultural frameworks. It touches on an individual's most basic fundamental beliefs. As a result, no one religion will ever be able to satisfy every person in the world.

WHERE WE ARE

As the twenty-first century unfolds, women are engaged in many different roles in religion. In some religions, such as Catholicism and Islam, rights have been limited. In other religions, such as some Protestant sects and certain divisions of Judaism, women have made tremendous gains in their right to contribute to worship services and serve as leaders in their churches. Many women have left organized religion completely and found the spirituality they seek in neopagan or alternative religions.

Those who are not happy with the status quo in their religions continue to work for a more equal place. The Women's Ordination Conference (WOC) is a voice for women in the

Masculine Language

The major Western religions all originated in male-oriented, patriarchal societies. As a result, the language used in these religions is masculine. God is "the Father" or "the king." Both God and Christ are male. This masculine language makes it difficult for some women to feel a connection with a religion where religious figures are always male. This can also have the effect of making women seem inferior by contrast.

In most cases, referring to gods and other religious figures as male is simply a fallback, since English lacks a pronoun that is not specifically male or female. However, many religions have interpreted this masculine language to mean that men are meant to be superior and women inferior.

Catholic Church. On March 25, 2009, it called for justice and equality in the Church on the World Day of Prayer:

> *Since 1975, WOC members have worked for women to be priests and for renewal of the priesthood. We have denounced the sexism that keeps women banned from ordination, while at the same time, we work to change church structures that are secretive, exclusive and lack transparency. Our aim is to restore the equality that Jesus and early church leaders modeled. For too long, only ordained, male, celibate clergy have dictated—or tried to dictate—how Catholics worship, pray and make decisions. This must change.*[1]

Other groups have formed in order to combat the feminist movement's attempts to change church structure. One such group is the Presbyterian Church of America (PCA), which is a conservative group. It split from the Presbyterian Church of the United States because it did not agree with the Presbyterian's liberal theological ideas and the placing of women in church leadership roles. At its annual General Assembly, the PCA voted against commissioning a study committee to examine women's roles in the denomination.

LOOKING TO THE FUTURE

Examining the roles that women will play in their respective religions in the future entails examining each religion individually. In some religions, such as Catholicism, decreasing numbers of priests might make it necessary to ordain women as priests. In recent years, the worldwide population of Catholics has been increasing. However, between 2007 and 2008 the number of priests available

Feminist Theology

As more women seek equality in religious roles, feminist theology is becoming increasingly important. It refers to practicing any theology from a feminist point of view, where both sexes are equal. Traditionally, religion and theology have been practiced from a male point of view.

One early attempt at feminist theology was Elizabeth Cady Stanton's *The Woman's Bible* in 1895. Stanton attempted to recast the Bible and the scriptures in a way that included women. Feminist theologians want religion to include the contributions and perspectives of women. They argue that feminist values such as reciprocity and acceptance are important values to add to these religions.

However, feminists approach religious reform in different ways. Some seek to work for female equality through the existing structure of the church. Others believe that the only way to practice feminist theology is through new churches that reject traditional male hierarchies. A third group agrees that many traditional religions are male oriented. However, times and customs have changed, and the male roles from the Bible should change as well. Even religions that have been reluctant to accept female equality are beginning to accept some aspects of feminist theology.

to minister to them decreased by approximately 2.5 percent. Many Catholic parishes have been forced to consolidate their congregations or share priests. Ordaining women as priests would help fill the gap. Yet the 2009 shift to allow Anglicans to join the Catholic Church could provide the needed male priests.

Still, in many churches, women outnumber men in membership. If the number of men actively involved in churches continues to decrease, it may become necessary to give women more power in order to keep churches vital and growing.

However, there are arguments against incorporating women into every aspect of certain religions. These arguments center on the need to maintain traditions and values that may be thousands of years old, such as in the case of Hasidic Judaism. Many worshipers feel that keeping women in their traditional roles, with an emphasis on the value of raising children and maintaining a religious home, helps to keep religions vital and passes along traditions and values intact. There are often other benefits as well. Stephanie Wellen Levine, author of *Mystics, Mavericks, and Merrymakers: An Intimate Journey Among Hasidic Girls,* found that most of the young Hasidic

A Hasidic girl prays in a graveyard in Cambria Heights, New York.

girls she interviewed did want to experience some
of the pleasures of secular U.S. culture. But on
the whole, the girls were unusually happy and had

a high level of self-esteem. Levine believes that these girls benefit from a religious community where there is no pressure about boys, dating, and other teen issues.

It is impossible to say whether the general trend toward equality in U.S. society will be applied to all religions in the future. Mary E. Hunt offered her opinion in her article "Women's History, Women's Future in Religion":

> In the [twentieth] century, virtually all religions were challenged from the inside out by their women members. Scholarship made it clear that women had been marginalized in most traditions. Opening theological and ministerial training to women meant women studied and were ordained in large numbers, now approaching a critical mass in many communities of faith. That work continues apace in most religious groups.[2]

Church Women United

In 1941, a group of 100 women from three different religious denominations met in Atlantic City, New Jersey, and formed Church Women United (CWU). Today, this group of Christian women includes members of Protestant, Roman Catholic, Orthodox, and other Christian religions who work together to grow in their faith and to serve their communities. Since its founding, CWU has worked to combat racism, promote diversity, and strengthen women's participation in the church. CWU was also active in the civil rights movement of the 1960s. Currently, there are more than a half million members.

A CELEBRATION OF SPIRITUALITY

On any given day in the United States, women practice their religions in a variety of ways. An Amish woman works in her garden, growing food for her family. A Muslim woman attends a business meeting, her hair covered by a hijab. A Jewish girl celebrates her bat mitzvah. A Catholic nun teaches a classroom full of children. And a young woman, a recent graduate from a seminary, is being ordained as a minister in a Protestant church. All of these women are following their religions, filling a role that is either as old as their faith itself or an adaptation to changing times.

Freedom of religion guarantees U.S. women the right to practice whatever religion they choose. As Susan Hill Lindley wrote,

> *The women's [religious] story is one of movement (sometimes two steps forward and one step back), a movement out of the subordinate female places [of early U.S. history]. Even those who see themselves as anti-feminist have accepted some of the gradual changes that have occurred during America's history.*[3]

Women in the United States can decide whether to seek equality with men in spiritual roles and decide what role to play by the way they practice their spirituality. However, many women continue to fight within their religions for greater rights. ⁓

Monica Myers is a pastor at Northwest Christian Church
in Seattle, Washington.

TIMELINE

1637	1656	early 1800s
Anne Hutchinson is put on trial and banished from the Massachusetts Bay Colony.	The first Quakers arrive in North America.	A series of religious movements called the Great Awakening occur in the United States.

1853	1875	1895
Antoinette Brown Blackwell becomes the first woman to be ordained as a Protestant minister.	Mary Baker Eddy forms the Christian Science Church.	Elizabeth Cady Stanton publishes the first volume of *The Woman's Bible*.

1809	1818	1848
Elizabeth Ann Seton forms the Sisters of Charity.	Jarena Lee begins preaching.	The Fox sisters hear mysterious rapping in their home; their experience begins the Spiritualist movement.

1912	1920	1922
Henrietta Szold forms the Hadassah organization for Jewish women.	The Nineteenth Amendment allows women the right to vote.	Judith Kaplan becomes the first U.S. Jewish girl to celebrate bat mitzvah.

TIMELINE

1923–1926	1941	1951
Aimee Semple McPherson preaches to crowds at her Angelus Temple in Los Angeles.	The Church Women United is organized.	Paula Ackerman becomes the first woman to perform the job of a rabbi.

1974	1974	1975
Selena Fox forms the Circle Sanctuary, a Wiccan church in Wisconsin.	Eleven female deacons are ordained in the Episcopal Church, against church policy.	Elizabeth Ann Seton is declared a saint by the Catholic Church.

1962–1965

Vatican Council II addresses the equality of women in the Catholic Church.

1968

Mary Daly's critique of the Catholic Church, *The Church and the Second Sex*, is published.

1972

Sally Jane Priesand becomes the first female officially ordained rabbi in the United States.

1989

Barbara Clementine Harris becomes the first female bishop in the Episcopal Church.

1994

Pope John Paul II declares that the Catholic Church lacks the authority to ordain women.

2009

The Vatican makes it easier for Anglicans to join the Catholic Church and become priests.

ESSENTIAL FACTS

AT ISSUE

In Favor of Traditional Roles

❖ Many conservative religions and organizations, such as the Council on Biblical Manhood and Womanhood, believe that if women are allowed leadership roles, the church and the family unit will be weakened.

❖ Catholics opposed to women priests point to interpretations of the Bible that seem to point to only men as church leaders.

❖ Religions, such as Hasidic Judaism, that assert women should fulfill traditional female roles often attempt to maintain honored traditions and values that may be thousands of years old.

In Favor of Leadership Roles

❖ Some Protestant denominations, such as Congregational and Episcopal, have followed societal trends and granted women more leadership positions.

❖ People in favor of women as priests in the Catholic Church point out that the number of Catholic priests is dwindling. Women may be needed to fill these positions.

❖ Some neopagans believe that all faiths are patriarchal and so have created their own religions that worship female deities and promote female leadership.

❖ Many Muslims, such as members of the Muslim Women's League, claim that interpretations of the Qur'an that place women as inferior to men and condone violence against women are invalid.

CRITICAL DATES

Early 1800s
The Great Awakening occurred in the United States and encouraged women to share their religious experiences and address social issues.

Mid-1800s
Spiritualism became a popular religious movement that encouraged female participation.

1895
Elizabeth Cady Stanton published *The Woman's Bible*.

Early 1900s
Women in some Protestant denominations were ordained as preachers or ministers. There were often restrictions on their roles.

1950s
Protestant women, particularly Methodists, Presbyterians, and Pentecostals, were allowed to preach with the same rights as male preachers.

1962–1969
Vatican II addressed the equality of women in the Catholic Church.

Quotes

"The Bible clearly teaches that men and women are equal in value and dignity and have distinct and complementary roles in the home and the church. If churches disregard these teachings and accommodate to the culture, then the members of those churches and subsequent generations will be less likely to submit to God's word in other difficult matters as well."—*Council on Biblical Manhood and Womanhood*

"The church influences society whether society acknowledges it or not. In fact, it has been suggested that no permanent social change takes place without a religious dimension. . . . When God, as interpreted by church action, says that women are the second order of creation, [women] are in real trouble."—*the Reverend Betty Bone Schiess*

ADDITIONAL RESOURCES

SELECT BIBLIOGRAPHY

Benowitz, June Melby. *Encyclopedia of American Women and Religion*. Santa Barbara, CA: ABC-CLIO, Inc., 1998.

Braude, Ann. *Women and American Religion*. New York, NY: Oxford University Press, 2000.

Diner, Hasia R., and Beryl Lieff Benderly. *Her Works Praise Her: A History of Jewish Women in America from Colonial Times to the Present*. New York, NY: Basic Books, 2002.

Lindley, Susan Hill. *"You have Stept out of your Place": A History of Women and Religion in America*. Louisville, KY: Westminster John Knox Press, 1996.

FURTHER READING

Avakian, Monique. *Reformers: Activists, Educators, Religious*. Austin, TX: Steck-Vaughn, 2000.

Bohannon, Lisa Frederiksen. *Women's Rights and Nothing Less: The Story of Elizabeth Cady Stanton*. Greensboro, NC: Morgan Reynolds, 2000.

Langley, Myrtle. *Religion*. New York, NY: Dorling Kindersley, 2005.

WEB LINKS

To learn more about women's roles in religion, visit ABDO Publishing Company online at **www.abdopublishing.com**. Web sites about women's roles in religion are featured on our Book Links page. These links are routinely monitored and updated to provide the most current information available.

For More Information

For more information on this subject, contact or visit the following organizations.

Glencairn Museum
1001 Cathedral Road, Bryn Athyn, PA 19009-0757
267-502-2993
www.glencairnmuseum.org
This museum educates visitors about the history of religion using art and artifacts.

National Women's History Museum
205 South Whiting Street, Suite 254, Alexandria, VA 22304
703-461-1920
www.nwhm.org
Founded in 1996, this museum is dedicated to preserving women's history.

International Museum of Muslim Cultures
Mississippi Arts Center, 201 East Pascagoula Street
Jackson, MS 39201
601-960-0440
www.muslimmuseum.org
This museum displays artifacts to educate people about Muslim culture and religion.

GLOSSARY

abolitionism
A movement to eliminate the practice of slavery in the United States.

burka
A loose garment that covers the entire body with only a veiled opening for the eyes, worn by Muslim women.

canonize
To make someone a saint.

catechism
A book containing a summary of the principles of a religion.

cloister
A place of religious seclusion, such as a convent or monastery.

congregation
A group of people who come together for religious worship.

denomination
A religious grouping, usually including many local churches and a ruling body.

evangelical
Emphasizing the teachings and authority of the scriptures.

excommunicate
To exclude or expel from church membership.

hierarchy
A ruling body of church clergy organized into ranks.

hijab
A traditional headscarf worn by Muslim women.

ordination
A ceremony or instance to make someone a priest or a minister.

pagan
Someone who practices a religion that is usually polytheistic or ancient and often connected to nature.

parish
> A denominational district having its own church and church official.

pastoral
> Having to do with the duties of a pastor or a minister.

patriarchal
> An organization where men and fathers have most of the power.

religious orders
> Men or women who take religious vows and often live in a communal setting.

Sabbath
> Saturday, the seventh day, and a day of religious observance for Jews and some Christians.

séance
> A meeting where a spiritualist tries to establish communication with the dead.

secular
> Relating to earthly or worldly life.

seminary
> A special school for education in theology and religious history, usually to prepare for the ministry.

subjection
> To bring someone under domination, influence, or control.

subordinate
> Belonging to a lower rank or order.

suffrage
> The right to vote and exercising that right.

temperance
> Abstinence from drinking alcoholic beverages.

theology
> The study of religious faith and practice, especially God and his relationship to the world.

SOURCE NOTES

Chapter 1. Women and Religion

1. June Melby Benowitz. *Encyclopedia of American Women and Religion*. Santa Barbara, CA: ABC-CLIO, Inc. 1998. ix.
2. Frederick W. Schmidt, Jr. *A Still Small Voice: Women, Ordination, and the Church*. Syracuse, NY: Syracuse University Press, 1996. x.

Chapter 2. Before the Twentieth Century

1. Susan Hill Lindley. *"You have Stept out of your Place": A History of Women and Religion in America*. Louisville, KY: Westminster John Knox Press, 1996. 5.
2. Ibid. 16.
3. Ann Braude. *Women and American Religion*. New York, NY: Oxford University Press, 2000. 45.

Chapter 3. Liberation and Changing Roles

1. Susan Hill Lindley. *"You have Stept out of your Place": A History of Women and Religion in America*. Louisville, KY: Westminster John Knox Press, 1996. 292.
2. Ibid. 299.
3. Ibid. 309–310.
4. Pope John XXIII. "Encyclical Letter On Establishing Universal Peace in Truth, Justice, Charity and Liberty." *Pacem in Terris (Peace on Earth): Encyclical Letter of Pope John XXIII on Establishing Universal Peace in Truth, Justice, Charity and Liberty Promulgated on 11 April 1963*. 11 Apr. 1963. *ewtn. com*. 24 July 2009 <www.ewtn.com/library/encyc/i23pacem.htm>.
5. Pope Paul VI. "Pastoral Constitution on the Church in the Modern World: Gaudium et Spes." 7 Dec. 1965. Vatican.va. 24 July 2009 <http://www.vatican.va/archive/hist_councils/ ii_vatican_council/documents/vat-ii_cons_19651207_gaudium-et-spes_en.html>.
6. Susan Hill Lindley. *"You have Stept out of your Place": A History of Women and Religion in America*. Louisville, KY: Westminster John Knox Press, 1996. 356.
7. Richard R. Melick, Jr. "Women Pastors: What Does the Bible Teach?" *Journal of the Southern Baptist Convention*. May 1998. *SBCLIFE.net*. 24 July 2009 <www.sbclife.net/articles/1998/05/sla5.asp>.

Chapter 4. Women and Protestantism

1. Sheri R. Benvenuti. "Pentecostal Women in Ministry: Where Do We Go From Here?" *Cyberjournal for Pentecostal-Charismatic Research*. 24 July 2009 <www.pctii.org/cyberj/cyberj1/ben.html>.
2. The Council on Biblical Manhood & Womanhood. "The Mission & Vision of CBMW." 2009. *CBMW.org*. 23 July 2009 <http://www.cbmw.org/Our-Mission-and-Vision>.
3. Ann Braude. *Women and American Religion*. New York, NY: Oxford University Press, 2000. 129.

Chapter 5. Women and Catholicism

1. Article #2258. *Catechism of the Catholic Church, Second Edition*. 24 July 2009 <www.scborromeo.org/ccc/p3s2c2a5.htm>.
2. Frederick W. Schmidt, Jr. *A Still Small Voice: Women, Ordination, and the Church*. Syracuse, NY: Syracuse University Press, 1996. 131.

Chapter 6. Women and Judaism

1. Allison Josephs. "Are Orthodox Jews Sexist?" *Jew in the City Online*. 29 July 2009. 3 Sept. 2009 <http://www.jewinthecity.com/a/2009/07/if-a-pictures-worth-a-thousand-words-how-about-a-video.html>.
2. Hasia R. Diner and Beryl Lieff Benderly. *Her Works Praise Her: A History of Jewish Women in America from Colonial Times to the Present*. New York, NY: Basic Books, 2002. 421.
3. Ann Braude. *Women and American Religion*. New York, NY: Oxford University Press, 2000. 102–103.

Chapter 7. Women and Islam

1. Saimah Ashraf. "Shattering Illusions: Western Conceptions of Muslim Women." *Jannah.org*. 24 July 2009 <http://www.jannah.org/sisters/shatter.html>.
2. Muslim Women's League. "Islamic Perspective on 'Honor Killings'." Apr. 1999. *mwlusa.org*. 18 Nov. 2009 <http://www.mwlusa.org/topics/violence&harrasment/hk.html>.
3. Tasleem K. Griffin. "Within the Sheltering Peace: Islam and Women." *2Muslims.com*. 24 July 2009 <http://www.2muslims.com/cgi-bin/links/page.cgi?page=print&link=222385>.

SOURCE NOTES CONTINUED

4. Naheed Mustafa. "My Body is My Own Business." *The Globe and Mail*. 29 June 1993. *Jannah.org*. 24 July 2009 <http://www.jannah.org/sisters/naheed.html>.
5. Dr. Sherif Abdel Azim. "Women in Islam Versus Women in the Judeo-Christina Tradition: The Myth and the Reality." *IslamiCity.com*. 24 July 2009. <http://www.islamicity.com/Articles/Articles.asp?ref=IC0301-2178>.

Chapter 8. Women and Alternative Religions
1. Ann Braude. *Women and American Religion*. New York: Oxford University Press, 2000. 126.
2. Margot Adler. "A Rainbow of Spirituality: Pagan and Wiccan Quotes and Guidance." 2007. *A-Rainbow-of-Spirituality.org*. 24 July 2009 <http://a-rainbow-of-spirituality.org/paganquotes.html>.
3. Carol P. Christ. "Why Women Need the Goddess." 1978. *Goddessariadne.org*. 24 July 2009 <http://www.goddessariadne.org/whywomenneedthegoddess.htm>.
4. James R. Lewis. *Witchcraft Today: An Encyclopedia of Wiccan and Neopagan Traditions*. Santa Barbara, CA: ABC-CLIO, Inc., 1999. 303.
5. Carol P. Christ. "Why Women Need the Goddess." 1978. *Goddessariadne.org* 24. July 2009 <http://www.goddessariadne.org/whywomenneedthegoddess.htm>.
6. Susan J. Palmer. *Moon Sisters, Krishna Mothers, Rajneesh Lovers: Women's Roles in New Religions*. Syracuse, NY: Syracuse University Press, 1994. 138–139.

Chapter 9. The Future of Women's Roles
1. "WOC Calls for Women's Justice and Equality in the Catholic Church on World Day of Prayer." 25 Mar. 2009. *WomensOrdination.org*. 24 July 2009 <http://www.womensordination.org/content/view/300/42>.
2. Mary E. Hunt. "Article of Faith: Women's History, Women's Future in Religion." *The Task Force National Religion Leadership Roundtable*. 24 July 2009 <http://www.thetaskforce.org/downloads/articles_of_faith/ArticleOfFaith_WomensHistoryWomensFuture.pdf>.
3. Susan Hill Lindley. *"You have Stept out of your Place": A History of Women and Religion in America*. Louisville, KY: Westminster John Knox Press, 1996. 434.

INDEX

INDEX CONTINUED

ABOUT THE AUTHOR

Marcia Amidon Lusted has written more than 25 books for young readers and numerous magazine articles. She is an instructor for the Institute of Children's Literature. She lives in New Hampshire with her family.

PHOTO CREDITS